ENERGY FILES

OIL & GAS

ENERGY FILES – OIL & GAS
was produced by

David West 👫 **Children's Books**
7 Princeton Court
55 Felsham Road
London SW15 1AZ

Editor: James Pickering
Picture Research: Carlotta Cooper

First published in Great Britain in 2002 by
Heinemann Library, Halley Court, Jordan Hill,
Oxford OX2 8EJ, a division of Reed Educational
and Professional Publishing Limited.

OXFORD MELBOURNE AUCKLAND
JOHANNESBURG BLANTYRE GABORONE
IBADAN PORTSMOUTH (NH) USA CHICAGO

Copyright © 2002 David West Children's Books

06 05 04 03 02
10 9 8 7 6 5 4 3 2 1

ISBN 0 431 15575 5 (HB)
ISBN 0 431 15582 8 (PB)

British Library Cataloguing in Publication Data

Parker, Steve, 1952 -
Oil & gas. - (Energy files)
1. Natural gas - Juvenile literature
2. Petroleum - Juvenile literature
I. Title
333.8'23

Printed and bound in Italy

PHOTO CREDITS :
Abbreviations: t-top, m-middle, b-bottom, r-right,
l-left, c-centre.

Front cover all - Corbis Images. 3, 4-5, 5 both, 7bl,
9bl, 10bl, 10-11t, 11 both, 12tl, 12-13t, 13bl, 14bl,
15ml & bl, 16tr & bl, 17br, 18bl, 18-19, 20-21
both, 21tl & bl, 22 both, 23mr & br, 25tl & mr,
26-27, 27bl, 28-29t, 29br, 30tr - Corbis Images.
6br (Adrian Arbib), 9br (John Isaac), 18br (Thoma
Raupach), 24bl (Mark Edwards), 26br (Jorgen
Schytte), 27br (Dylan Garcia), 30ml (Pierre Gleizes
- Still Pictures. 8bl, 12br, 13tr, 14tr & br, 15mr,
17tr, 26bl, 27tr, 30bl - Katz/FSP. 12bl - Spectrum
Colour Library. 20bl, 21mr - Castrol. 21tr - S.
Keep/Robert Harding Picture Library. 23tr - Rex
Features. 25bm - British Plastics Foundation. 28-
29b, 29tr - Hitachi.

*An explanation of difficult words can be
found in the glossary on page 31.*

ENERGY FILES

OIL & GAS

Steve Parker

Heinemann
LIBRARY

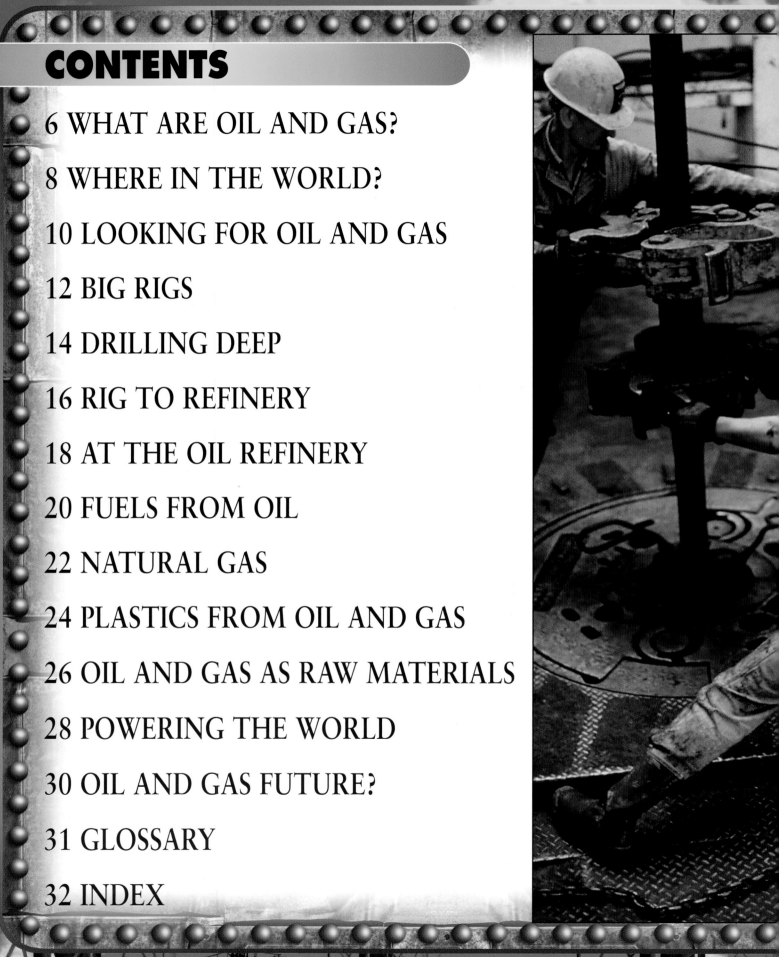

CONTENTS

INTRODUCTION

Oil, petroleum, crude, 'black gold' – this dark, thick goo is one of the world's most valuable resources. It is our most vital source of energy, processed into petrol, diesel and other fuels for millions of trucks, planes, ships, cars, power stations, furnaces, boilers and heating systems. It is also a raw material for plastics, paints and countless other products. The oil business dominates our modern world.

Workers on a rig (left) join sections of a drill 'string', to bore deep into the earth and tap new oil supplies.

Oil is split into its many constituents – separate parts – at refineries (above). These are some of the globe's biggest industrial sites.

Some supertankers weigh more than half a million tonnes. They carry whole 'lakes' of oil from natural fields to ports and cities.

WHAT ARE OIL AND GAS?

Many millions of years ago, dinosaurs ruled the world. In the seas lived tiny plants and animals, microscopic in size, and very similar to the plankton in the oceans today. Oil and gas are made from those tiny plants and animals.

Oil collects and moves in porous rock, like water in a sponge.

HOW OIL AND GAS FORMED

Ooze on the ancient sea bed, containing trillions of tiny dead bodies, was slowly 'pressure-cooked' by heat and weight as more layers piled up on top.

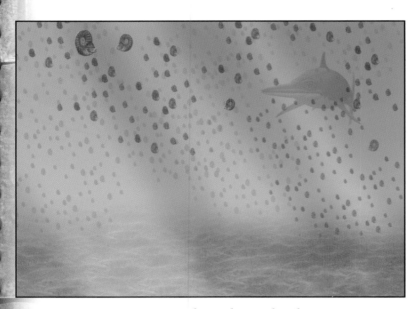

Ancient seas swarmed with a plankton 'soup', through which swam creatures like ammonites.

1 Tiny living things in the sea died and sank.

2 More layers built up, with pressure and heat at about 80–100°C.

In some places, pools of oil and tar seep up on to the ground. Most of these surface deposits were used up long ago.

DEATH BED

The mini-plankton of prehistoric seas died in their trillions and sank to the sea bed, and were buried in the mud. More tiny dead bodies 'rained' down on top. Over immense time in the depths, they were squashed, heated and part-rotted to form oil and gas.

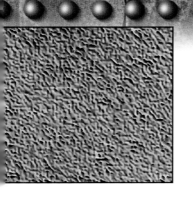

TRACED BACK TO THE SUN

Oil and gas contain chemical energy, in the links or 'bonds' between their tiny particles, atoms. Animals in the original plankton got this energy by eating plants, which in turn obtained it from sunlight (like plants today). So oil and gas are stored Sun's energy.

The dead bodies partly decayed into a thick liquid, giving off gas bubbles as they rotted. This oil and gas, being lighter than the water in the rock, seeped up through tiny holes or pores. They were stopped by a 'trap' of non-porous (completely solid) rock above. Salty water and earth movements moved the oil and gas into their final trapped positions.

3 Oil and gas formed and seeped upwards under non-porous rock.

4 A salt dome split the oil and gas reservoir.

5 Earth movements cracked and folded the rock layers.

Gas

Oil

Water

An oil well in a corn field.

 Green **ISSUES**

Oil and gas occur under all kinds of land (and the sea bed). Drilling holes to extract them may not cause too much disturbance on ordinary farmland. But in nature reserves, wildlife parks and areas of natural beauty, the drill towers, pipes, roads, noise and disturbance can greatly harm the environment.

WHERE IN THE WORLD?

Oil and gas occur in more than half of the countries in the world. But many of these stores, or reserves, are small and patchy. The biggest and most worthwhile oil fields are in the Middle East, the largest gas fields in Russia.

AROUND THE WORLD

The oil business began almost 150 years ago in eastern North America, providing fuel for lamps and oil-burning heaters. As motor vehicles spread, from the 1890s, the need for petrol boosted the industry. Huge oil fields were discovered in Texas (USA) and the Middle East in the 1930s, and in Alaska and Russia from the 1960s. The 1990s saw more discoveries in Siberia.

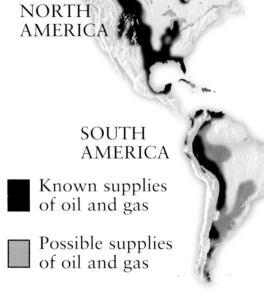

NORTH AMERICA

SOUTH AMERICA

■ Known supplies of oil and gas

□ Possible supplies of oil and gas

There are known or 'proved' oil and gas fields in many parts of the world. There are also new areas to explore, where oil and gas will probably be found.

Oil companies deal with vast amounts of money. Their head offices are often huge skyscrapers – like the world's tallest, the Petronas Towers in Kuala Lumpur, Malaysia

Oil is also locked up mountainous rocks, 'shales' in the US states Colorado, Wyoming and Utah. This oil is cost and difficult to extra

RUSSIA

JROPE

RICA   SOUTH EAST ASIA

MIDDLE
EAST

AUSTRALIA

OIL RESERVES TODAY

The Middle East has more than two-thirds of the world's known oil reserves. One nation, Saudi Arabia, has one quarter of the total. Next come Central and South America, then Africa, Russia and North America about equal, South East Asia and Australia, and Europe. Oil is measured in barrels. Saudi Arabia has 260,000 million barrels, Europe 19,000 million.

Green ISSUES

Oil is so valuable that nations have gone to war over it. In 1990, Iraq invaded its tiny neighbour, Kuwait, and tried to take over its oil fields. During the Gulf War that followed, many oil fields were deliberately set on fire, and oil slicks leaked into the sea, with immense damage to the environment.

Oil fields blaze during the Gulf War, 1991.

The rewards of finding new oil and gas fields are huge. An army of surveyors, geologists and other experts constantly search, or prospect, for them with the latest high-technology gadgets.

IN THE AIR

There are many surface clues to oil or gas under the ground, and some of these can be detected from the air or even space. The shapes of hills and valleys, colours of bare rock, and even how much heat it soaks up from the Sun, all help to identify the age and type of rock, and if oil is likely below.

THE SEARCH FOR CLUES

Satellite images (1), aerial photograph (2) and radar (3) give increasingly accurate surface maps. Small test-explosions or 'thumpers' on land (4) and at sea (5) send shock or seismic waves through the rocks, to be detected and analysed (6, 7).

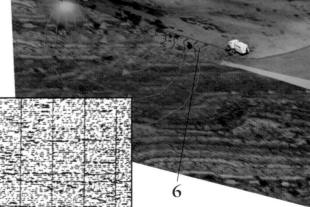

The surface is lifeless and without promise, yet riches lie just below, in Middle East deserts.

Seismometers trace out shock waves altered by passing through rock layers.

IN THE GROUND

Geophysical studies use ground-penetrating radar, which shows layers of rocks and where one type changes to another, metres beneath the surface. Lasers measure how rocks shake like jelly after test explosions.

On land (8) and at sea (9), sensitive devices called gravimeters and magnetometers detect variations in Earth's gravity and magnetism caused by rocks below.

Tiny amounts of gas bubbling from the sea bed are sensed by a 'sniffer' which checks for various chemicals (10). If all the clues point to gas or oil below, test-drilling is carried out by small rigs, into the ground (11), or at sea (12) by an offshore exploration platform.

3

2

9

1

7

5

10

12

Geologists test samples of rocks for their mineral contents.

11

BIG RIGS

Reaching oil and gas is 'boring' work. Holes are bored or drilled into the earth, to allow them to flow out.

Hundreds of workers live on offshore rigs.

PARTS OF THE RIG

A drilling rig has several parts. The wide, flat base is called a platform. The tower is known as a derrick. The drill itself is a long series of steel pipes, called a string, tipped by a cutting bit (see page 15). There are many designs of rigs, depending on their location – on land, inshore or offshore.

Rarely, rigs suffer accidents such as storm damage. Some have been sunk on purpose in deep water (right), at the end of their working lives.

ALL AT SEA

Inshore, a fixed-leg rig (1) can stand on the sea bed, on its stilt-like legs. The greatest water depth for these rigs is about 400 metres.

Divers check a rig under water.

Ocean rigs have two 'lifelines'. Helicopters are used for emergencies and staff transport, and ships for routine supplies such as food and equipment.

...he floating rig has ...ant buoyancy tanks ...lled with air or oil (2). ... may be tied by cables ... blocks on the sea ...ed, as a tension-leg rig.

Tension-leg rigs work in water up to 1,000 metres deep. Farther out, the rig ship (3) is kept still, 'on station', by anchors, thrusters (propellers in various directions) and satellite navigation.

Green ISSUES

Ocean rigs are exposed, isolated places, and their work with oil and gas involves many hazards. In the North Sea in 1988, the Piper Alpha platform suffered a gas leak and serious fire, and 167 people died – the world's worst rig tragedy. It was followed by many improvements in safety.

Piper Alpha blazes, North Sea.

The 'nodding donkey' is a small production unit that lifts or sucks up oil, day and night.

EXPLORE, PRODUCE

The first big arrivals at a possible new oil or gas field are exploratory rigs. They drill more test bores to check the depth of the field and how far it extends. If the field is worth tapping, more holes are bored for production wells. A production platform, without a derrick, may replace the exploratory rig, which moves to the next site.

13

The cutting edge of the oil and gas industry is the bit. At the tip of the drill string 'daisy chain', it spins and grinds its way through thousands of metres of solid rock.

HOW THE DRILL WORKS

The drill string is made of lengths of pipe screwed together. As the cutting bit at the lower end bores deeper, more lengths are added at the upper end. In a rotary drill the whole string spins, clamped into and driven by the platform turntable (rotary table), powered by diesel engines.

It's a blow-out! In many fields, oil is under huge pressure, deep in the rocks. It may blast through the taps and valves of a well head.

The platform turntable is stopped while a new section (length) of pipe is added to the drill string.

Green ISSUES

A blow-out (above) not only wastes valuable oil, it also pollutes the surroundings. Special equipment is needed to 'cap' the well and control the flow. Legendary oil man 'Red' Adair was called upon to cap many troublesome blow-outs around the world.

Oil-capper 'Red' Adair

Control room

Derrick

Cables

Turntable

Mud pump

1

In directional drilling (1), the bit spins as the string stays still. The bit is turned by mud, pumped at high pressure down the string pipe to a spiral motor near the end (2). The mud also cools the bit and carries drilled-off rock back to the surface. The bit is tilted at a slight angle to cut a curve. The production string (3) has holes allowing the oil to flow in.

Mud pipe

Blow-out valve at well head

Drill string

Mud flows up around string to surface.

Sections of pipe wait their turn to join the drill string.

Information from sensors in the drill string and bit is fed to the control room.

Mud flows down pipe string to bit.

Drill force sensors

Drill direction sensors

Collars prevent string buckling.

3

Oil out

Oil

Gas

Well perforations

Water

2

Mud spray cools and flushes rock pieces from spinning bit.

Drill bits tipped with diamond dust.

Mud-powered spiral motor

Rock temperature and hardness sensors

RIG TO REFINERY

Oil and gas are found in many remote places, from frozen polar lands to the steamy tropics. They must be transported to the refineries, to be turned into fuels and products.

A big tanker may bring enough oil, in one load, to supply a large city with enough fuels for more than one year.

OVER THE LAND

About two-thirds of all oil comes from under the ground. Being a liquid, it can be forced by powerful pumps along a pipeline laid on the surface or buried below. Booster or relay pumps give an extra push every few dozen kilometres.

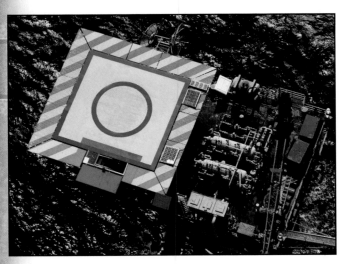

Some production rigs are automatic, without staff. Helicopters visit at intervals, for checks and maintenance.

OVER AND UNDER THE SEA

Mooring buoy
Giant tankers tie up to a floating buoy, which has its own helipad, and wait to be loaded.

LPG (liquid petroleum gas)
Natural gas is squeezed into a liquid in huge spheres, to reduce its volume greatly.

Oil storage
Oil flows from wells continuously. It is stored in massive containers called cells fixed to the sea bed, away from wave and storm damage.

Thick, gooey oil flows very slowly, especially in cold places where low temperatures make it thicker. It may be more efficient to pipe it into a supertanker, for a journey by sea. Oil and gas from offshore platforms are also loaded into tankers. Inshore platforms near refineries have their own pipelines.

Refinery
A tanker fills enormous storage cells and sets off again.

Undersea pipeline
If an oil field is large enough, it has its own pipeline and refinery built nearby. Small fields usually have tanker transport.

Unloading
Oil refineries need plenty of mooring space. Supertankers take 20 km to turn around or stop.

The longest overland pipeline is 3,787 km, across North America.

Green ISSUES

Oil sometimes spills by accident from a pipe or tanker. At sea, it floats as a thick black slick. This can devastate sea life such as birds and fish for many years in the future.

Rescuing an oiled guillemot.

17

Crude oil (petroleum) straight from the ground is not a single substance. It is a mixture of many hundreds of different substances.

HEATED

The refinery's main job is to separate these many different substances, or constituents. This is done using heat and pressure. At high temperatures, most of the constituents of crude oil turn into gases and vapours. These are led along a main pipe into a very tall fractionation tower, or column, which may be more than 100 metres high.

The refinery is a giant maze of pipes, tubes, tower and tanks, working all day and night. Some products from refined oil are re-heated to separate them further. Others are re-mixed or blended to make special products like kerosene for jet engines.

Green ISSUES

Many of oil's products are fuels, for burning in boilers or engines. These very hazardous chemicals are stored in refinery tanks before being collected by tankers. Despite many safety features, accidents may happen, with leaks, fires and explosions.

Monitors check the refining process.

Refinery fire in Hamburg, Germany.

COOLED

In the fractionation tower, the vapours and gases cool and turn back into liquids. But different levels in the tower are at different temperatures, so the separate substances turn back into liquids in different places.

FRACTIONS OF OIL

The fractionation tower is hot at the bottom and cooler at the top. A complex mixture of gases and vapours from heated crude oil enter and rise. The lightest gases leave at the top. Slightly heavier ones condense (turn into liquid) just below, and so on. The thickest, heaviest substances are drained off from the base of the tower. The products obtained at each level are called fractions.

Gases for bottled fuels (propane, butane)

Coolest part of tower

Solvents and chemicals for industry

30°C

Light fuels (paraffin, kerosene)

Medium fuels (petrol)

Heavy fuels (diesel, heating oils)

Chemicals

Light lubricating oils

Heavy fuel oils (ships, heating)

400°C

Vapours and gases from heated crude oil

Hottest part of tower

Thick lubricating oils and waxes

Tars, bitumens, pitches, asphalts

FUELS FROM OIL

Around the world, about one-third of all the oil which comes out of the ground is used to make fuels for transport. We put them into cars, trucks, ships, trains and planes.

PETROL POWER

Most car engines run on petrol (gasoline). This is the single biggest, most important product made from oil. Even though petrol is obtained by refining oil, it is not a pure substance. It is a complex mixture of many substances – chiefly hydrocarbons, which are chemicals made from hydrogen and carbon. A tank of petrol releases ten times more heat energy, when burned, as a pile of coal of the same weight.

Filling up with petrol is a regula chore of modern life. But petro is not a renewable energy sourc

NO OIL, NO GO

Vehicles such as cars rely on oil – and not just for fuel, as petrol. Nearly all the other fluids in the car, including lubricants for the gears and other moving parts, are made from crude oil. So are greases and the hydraulic (pressure) fluids for the suspension and brakes.

Petrol
Gearbox oil
Engine oil
Brake hydraulic fluid
Lubricating grease

Green ISSUES

Exhaust fumes from vehicles contain chemicals such as oxides of sulphur. Diesel exhausts also give off tiny specks, particulates. These substances collect in calm, sunny weather over traffic-choked cities and form smog, which causes breathing difficulties and other health problems.

Smog = bad health.

Diesel is similar to petrol but fuels bigger engines in trucks and tractors.

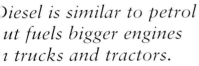

Fuels used by specialist vehicles, like racing cars, are continually improved to release more of their chemical energy as heat, while causing less engine wear.

Pound for pound, a commercial airliner uses less fuel, and is more economical than a family car.

21

Natural 'gas' is really natural 'gases'. Like oil, these formed deep in the ground, and they are separated and purified at a refinery.

SMELLY GAS

In most gas fields, about nine-tenths is the gas methane. This is the substance also given off by rotting food, compost

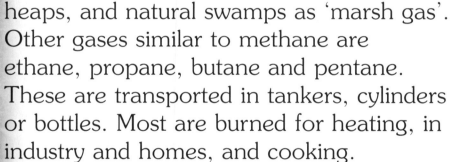

heaps, and natural swamps as 'marsh gas'. Other gases similar to methane are ethane, propane, butane and pentane. These are transported in tankers, cylinders or bottles. Most are burned for heating, in industry and homes, and cooking.

Natural gas varies in its make-up. As it arrives by pipeline it is checked for 'slugs' – when there is too much of an unwanted gas such as carbon dioxide. Then methane is separated by pressure and temperature, and piped separate.

Pockets of unwanted gases, called 'slugs', are removed by slug-catcher units before refining.

2 Slug catcher

1 Natural gas pipeline

5 Bulk methane is also cooled into liquid and shipped by special liquid natural gas (LNG) tankers.

A gas refinery yields fuels to burn and raw materials for industry.

6 Non-methane gases are sent fractionating columns for separation.

The non-methane gases pass to tall fractionating towers, where they are heated and cooled as in an oil refinery. The purified gases can be collected by ship or road. Propane is burned for home central heating; butane is popular for camping stoves.

Safety ISSUES

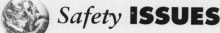

Some gases in natural gas have no smell, making it difficult to 'sniff' a leak. A substance with a distinct odour may be added to the gas, so users can smell any escape or other problem.

A gas leak causes a blaze at a refinery.

Ball-shaped storage tanks resist the great pressure of the gas inside, without cracks or splits.

3 Bulk methane is separated from other gases.

4 Bulk methane is delivered for direct burning by pipeline network.

10 Remaining gases are used as mixed fuels or by chemical industry.

9 Propane and butane are collected by ship or truck.

8 Propane and butane are pressurized for storage in spherical tanks.

7 Ethane is taken by road tankers for chemical industry.

Road tankers visit the refinery non-stop. Their hazardous loads must be identified with warning symbols.

23

About one-third of oil is used, not for energy, but as a raw material for industry. Some of the main products made from oil and gas are plastics.

Ethylene

Polyethylene

Hydrogen atom   Carbon atom   Chemical bond

PLASTICS GALORE

There are hundreds of kinds of plastics making countless goods, from children's toys to the parts in high-speed engines. Most plastics are produced by heating various refined substances from oil with other chemicals such as catalysts.

MAKING PLASTICS

The simple chemical ethylene (ethene, left) is found in natural gas. It has six units or atoms – two carbons and four hydrogens. Heated and squeezed with other chemicals, the simple monomers (see next page) join into a long polymer chain.

1 Monomers are warmed into liquid form in stir tanks.

2 Monomers link into longer polymers in reactor vessel.

Coolers

Heaters

3 Hot liquid plastic is forced along a tube at high pressure by a screw extruder.

Oil is used to make certain artificial fibres, such as polyester for clothing.

Plastic components cool after shaping on a production line.

...thylene monomers link to ...orm polyethylene, which is a ...pe of relatively soft, flexible ...astic (also called polythene) ...sed to make wrapping and ...ags. Polyethylene can also ...e further treated to make ...olyvinyl chloride, better ...nown as the plastic PVC. ...ther monomers make ...ifferent types of plastics.

...Plastic is ...ooled, hardened ...d cut into ...hips.

...old ...ater in

Squirt and suck

Most plastics, in their chemical make-up, are known as polymers. They are formed of many single units, monomers, joined together in long chains, like beads on a necklace. The joining is carried out by heat and pressure. Raw plastic from the factory is mixed with pigments (colouring) and heated, pressed and squirted into moulds, or sucked into hollow shapes, to make the final products.

Green ISSUES

Plastics, rubbers and similar oil-based products are useful partly because they are not 'biodegradable'. They do not rot away or decay naturally. However, this causes huge problems of waste disposal. Recycling is difficult for some plastics and rubbers; burning them releases harmful fumes.

A problem here to stay.

Warmed water out

Chip cutter

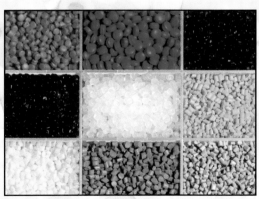

Raw plastic is coloured with pigments, ready for shaping.

Plastic products are mostly safe, strong, hard-wearing and wipe-clean.

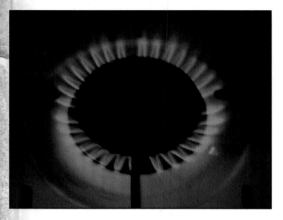

Only about one-hundredth of all gas is burned in homes, for cooking and heating.

Wherever you are – home or school, office or factory, in a car or train or plane, at the mall – items made from oil and gas are all around.

PETROCHEMICALS

After oil and gas are refined to make fuels, there are many substances left over. They are the basis of the giant petrochemicals industry. For example, natural gas contains sulphur and nitrogen chemicals, which can be processed into valuable fertilizers that add goodness to the soil.

Bags of chemical fertilizers, which are used to enrich the soil and keep crop production high.

Safety ISSUES

Gas is a relatively clean, efficient fuel. But if it leaks and there's a spark nearby – BOOM. Despite many safety precautions, each year there are several accidental gas explosions in homes, factories and industrial sites.

Result of a gas blast.

Vehicles can be adjusted to run on gas fuel. But the gas is stored under great pressure in a strong tank, which raises safety issues.

...all towers house 'cracking' units, where refined oil chemicals are broken apart further, into simpler substances.

Paints contain solvents, pigments and fillers – all made from oil.

CRACKING OIL

Substances from the refined oil and gas are further changed by cracking – heating under pressure with various chemicals. The results make an almost endless list of products – dyes, soaps, shampoos, cleaning fluids, artificial rubbers, solvents, pesticides, herbicides, cosmetics …

Gas burns fairly 'clean', with fewer fumes and particles compared to petrol or diesel, making it a useful fuel in busy cities.

POWERING THE WORLD

The main single use of oil and gas is for power – to make electricity. They are burned as fuels in power stations to release their energy as heat.

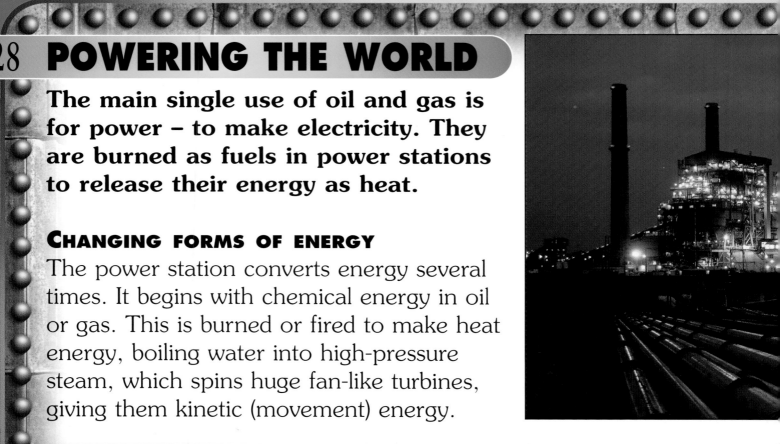

CHANGING FORMS OF ENERGY

The power station converts energy several times. It begins with chemical energy in oil or gas. This is burned or fired to make heat energy, boiling water into high-pressure steam, which spins huge fan-like turbines, giving them kinetic (movement) energy.

THE POWER STATION

Oil or gas burn to release heat, turning the turbines with their sets of angled blades (like the Hitachi turbine, right). Also on the turbine shaft are huge wire coils, the rotor, which spin in magnetism made by the stator around them. When a wire moves in a magnetic field, electricity flows, and is led away from the rotor.

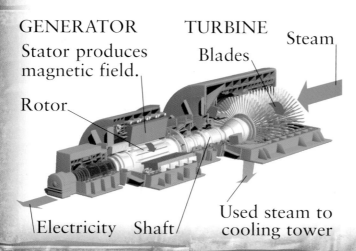

GENERATOR
Stator produces magnetic field.

Rotor

Electricity   Shaft

TURBINE
Blades

Steam

Used steam to cooling tower

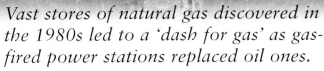

Vast stores of natural gas discovered in the 1980s led to a 'dash for gas' as gas-fired power stations replaced oil ones.

ELECTRICAL POWER

The spinning turbines are linked to a generator. This is the last stage in the energy chain, converting movement, with the help of powerful magnetism, into electricity.

Around the world, oil-fired power stations produce one-eighth of all electricity. Gas-fired stations make more, about one-sixth, for less overall pollution. But these amounts vary hugely. By far the most oil-thirsty nation is the USA, making more than one-third of its electricity from this source.

Modern gas-fired power plants like Hitachi's Goldendale HRSG use new 'combined cycle' technology. The gas is fired for a first turbine and generator, then the hot waste gases boil water into steam for a second turbine and generator.

Green ISSUES

Most electricity is made by burning three fossil fuels – oil, gas and coal. Stores of these are running down fast. Also, as they burn, they release many kinds of pollution, as well as greenhouse gases which are causing the world to get warmer.

Electricity comes – but at a price.

OIL AND GAS FUTURE?

Oil and gas are fossil fuels, and so non-renewable. We use them fast but they are not being replaced. So how long will they last, and can we use less of them, to make them go further?

Oil shales (see pages 8–9) may be extracted from rocks when supplies run low in the future.

Plant oils can be used as fuels.

WORLD STORES

If we keep using oil and gas at today's rates, gas may run out in 80 years, and oil in perhaps less than 60 years. New reserves are still being found, so these times may become longer. But in the end we must develop renewable energy supplies and use less energy all round.

OIL AND GAS RESERVES

Supporters of oil and gas say there are more reserves now than 20 years ago – but only because new fields have been discovered.

Such discoveries cannot continue for ever. The nations which use most oil, such as the USA, can help by cutting back the most.

Oil and its uses are major global issues.

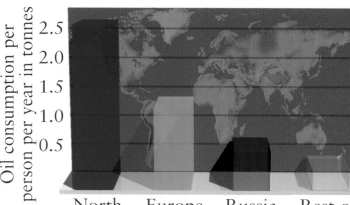

Oil consumption per person per year in tonnes

2.5
2.0
1.5
1.0
0.5

North America   Europe   Russia   Rest of World

GLOSSARY

drill string
Many drill pipes joined in a long line, usually by screwing together, with the cutting bit at the end.

geologist
An expert on the Earth, especially its rocks and minerals, and how these are made and change.

geophysical
The physical features of rocks and minerals, such as their hardness, colour and crystal shapes (rather than their chemical features such as whether they are acidic).

onshore
At sea, but relatively near the shore or coastline, where the water is not too deep, usually 0–250 metres.

laser
A special kind of light which is very powerful, with a pure colour, and shines in a narrow beam. Lasers are used for measuring, cutting and many other purposes.

offshore
In the open ocean, away from the shore or coastline, where the water is very deep.

prospecting
Looking or searching, usually for Earth's mineral resources such as oil, gas, coal, metals, crystals or gemstones (jewels).

radar
A system for detecting objects or layers, by beaming out invisible radio waves and measuring the way these are altered or reflected (bounced back).

salt dome
Salt minerals which flow slowly at high temperature and pressure, into a balloon or umbrella shape, often found near oil and gas fields.

satellite navigation
Locating your position using the signals beamed out by satellites in space, detected by a GPS (global positioning system) receiver.